WRITE NOW!

It's Never Too Late

Julie Belmont

Night Raven Publishing

Copyright © 2025 by Julie Belmont

All rights reserved.

No portion of this book may be reproduced in any form without written permission from the publisher or author, except as permitted by U.S. copyright law.

This publication is designed to provide accurate and authoritative information regarding the subject matter covered. It is sold with the understanding that neither the author nor the publisher is engaged in rendering legal, investment, accounting, or other professional services. While the publisher and author have used their best efforts in preparing this book, they make no representations or warranties with respect to the accuracy or completeness of the contents of this book and specifically disclaim any implied warranties of merchantability or fitness for a particular purpose. The advice and strategies contained herein may not be suitable for your situation. You should consult with a professional when appropriate. Neither the publisher nor the author shall be liable for any loss of profit or any other commercial damages, including but not limited to special, incidental, consequential, personal, or other damages.

Book Cover by Julie Belmont

2025

ISBN: 978-0-9755984-4-3

Night Raven Publishing

Also by Julie Belmont

Please visit me at website below:

Enjoy, and thank you for your interest and support.

https://www.juliebelmont.com/books.html

Self-help:

WRITE NOW! It's Never Too Late

The Path to Personal Success and Freedom

Creativity Business Plan for Artist sand Artists at Heart

Live the Life you Love Series, Seizing your Success

Children's books:

Chloe's Journey (Illustrated Children's book)

Novels:

Bad Blood in the Bayou-An LA to LA Cozy Mystery Book 1

'FRAMED'

Bad Blood in the Bayou-An LA to LA Cozy Mystery Book 2

'WIDE-ANGLE'

Upcoming Release in 2025

Next Book in the Series—in the works, Bad Blood in the Bayou-'FREEZE FRAME'

An LA to LA Cozy Mystery Book 3

If this book lights a creative spark in you, don't keep it a secret
leave a review and pass the spark along!"
Thank you

Contents

Introduction	VIII
PART I:	1
Chapter 1 Your Age Is Your Superpower	3
Chapter 2 Silencing the Inner Heckler	7
Chapter 3 Writing Isn't a Youth Sport	15
PART II:	21
1. Chapter 4 Claiming Your Time and Space	23
2. Chapter 5 Tools of the Trade (That Won't Make You Feel Lost or Left Behind)	29

3. Chapter 6   35
Writing Through Real Life

4. PART III: 43

5. Chapter 7   45
What do you want to write?

6. Chapter 8   53
From Idea to Outline (or Not)

7. Chapter 9   61
The First Draft: Ugly or Not

8. Chapter 10   67
Editing without Tears

9. PART IV: 75

10. Chapter 11   77
To Publish or Not to Publish?

11. Chapter 12   87
Navigating the Publishing World (Even if You Detest Social Media)

12. Chapter 13   93
Rejection, Reviews, and Not Giving a Care

13. PART V: 99

14. Chapter 14   101
Writing and Wellness

15. Chapter 15   107
Staying Inspired When Life Gets Loud

16. Chapter 16   113
Your Legacy in Words

About the author   117

Acknowledgements   119

A Note to you, the Writer   121

Introduction

> "You are never too old to set another goal or to dream a new dream."
>
> — *C.S. Lewis*

You're Not Too Old, and It's Not Too Late

Let's get one thing straight right out of the gate: writing isn't a young person's game. It's a human one. And if you're holding this book, you've got the most important thing any writer needs. Curiosity, imagination, and the desire to do something creative.

You've lived. You've lost. You've laughed, struggled, wandered, come back. Maybe you've raised families, run businesses, changed careers—maybe you're still doing all that and trying to sneak in writing on the side. Or maybe you're finally at a point in life where there's time to breathe, think, and create.

Either way, you're not starting from scratch. You're starting from **experience**. And that's your gold mine.

This book isn't about writing *like* you're younger. It's about writing *because* you're not. Because you know what matters. Because you're done waiting for permission. Because it's finally time to say what's been sitting inside you for too long.

I've designed this guide to walk you through the full writing journey—from idea to execution, from "maybe someday" to "I actually did this." And if you've never written before, don't worry. I'll meet you exactly where you are—no jargon, no judgment, no talking down.

We'll talk honestly about the challenges: procrastination, perfectionism, feeling like the publishing world doesn't speak your language. We'll also cover the good stuff: tools that make your writing life easier, ways to get unstuck, how to create stories or books that matter to *you*—and maybe to the world.

I'll be talking to you from the heart. I'm of a certain age and have moved forward into a place of comfort when it comes to writing. I've been writing in one way or another for many years, but there is something different about writing, like nobody is watching. Putting down ideas and reaching out to help others embark on a rewarding journey, not just financially, but fulfilling to one's soul.

Connecting heart and mind is one of the practices we'll be discussing. Using experiences, memories, and emotions, and combining them with logical and tactical elements to create a cohesive whole.

I want to share that with you so that you can do the same. Nothing can stop us from moving forward in the next chapter of our creative adventure. You'll find examples, inspiration, and practical strategies for moving forward, no matter how late you think you're starting.

Spoiler alert: It's not late. It's right on time. So, let's begin. You've got something to say. Let's write it down.

"It's never too late—in fiction or in life—to revise."
— Nancy Thayer

PART I:

MINDSET MAKEOVER-
GETTING OUT OF YOUR OWN WAY

Chapter 1
Your Age Is Your Superpower

Let's flip the script on what you've been told.

Society loves to hand out expiration dates like coupons. And nowhere does that nonsense show up more than in the arts—especially writing. They celebrate the hotshot 23-year-old with a six-figure book deal while giving the side-eye to someone over fifty who dares to put pen to paper. Newsflash: youth is not a requirement. Talent, persistence, perspective, and courage are.

Guess what you've got?

All four.

You've lived long enough to know that life isn't a straight line. You've gathered stories, wisdom, and grit. You've experienced change, loss, triumph, and transformation. Every single one of those moments are yours to evaluate and make them worth something. You've gained enough life experience to realize that life is full of twists and turns. You've accumulated stories, wisdom, and strength throughout your journey. You've navigated change, loss, triumph, and transformation. Each of these experiences is invaluable—raw material for memoirs, fiction, and essays, creating characters that are far more profound and compelling than anything a recent graduate with a creative writing degree could conceive.

What Age *Really* Brings to the Page

Let's break it down. Here's what you've got that younger writers are still earning:

- **Voice.** Not the squeaky, unsure kind. A real, developed, lived-in voice. That's rare—and powerful.

- **Perspective.** You've got context. You've seen how life loops back on itself. You understand nuance, contradiction, and gray areas.

- **Stamina (Yes, Really).** You've done hard things. Writing is just another one—and frankly, it's easier than surviving your twenties.

- **No Time for Nonsense.** You're less likely to second-guess every comma or stall out because of what someone might think. You know how to push through doubt.

- **A Desire to *Do the Darn Thing*.** You're here because something inside you said, "It's time." That voice doesn't mess around.

But... What If I've Never Done This Before?

Even better. No bad habits to unlearn. No old MFA (Master of Fine Arts) baggage. No tortured sense of literary ego. Just a clean slate, a clear head, and a lifetime of stories waiting to be written down. You're not starting late. You're starting right.

Think of this chapter as a reframing. You're not at a disadvantage—you're holding a pen powered by lived experience. And that ink flows deeper than most.

Let Me Say It Plain:

This book isn't here to coddle you. It's here to equip you. Your age doesn't disqualify you—it *qualifies* you. So, when that voice pops up whispering, "Who am I to write a book at this age?"—you answer it with this:

"I am someone who has earned the right to speak."

And then you go write it—with purpose, with power, and without hesitation. This book is not a fiction novel that you immerse yourself in to escape from a mundane existence or to relax, enjoy, and dream along with the characters. This is a short book designed to gently encourage you to act. I'm here to motivate you and show you the tools needed to realize your dream as the writer that you are.

Optional Writing Prompt (Soft Sidebar)

Quick Prompt: Think of one life experience that shaped who you are today. It doesn't have to be a headline event—just something that stayed with you. Jot down what happened, how you felt, and what it taught you. Now ask yourself: *Could this become a story? A scene? A lesson for someone else?*

Chapter 2
Silencing the Inner Heckler

(Or at least turning the volume way, way down)
Shut down fear, imposter syndrome, and all those "too late" lies.

You know that voice. We all do. It's the one that shows up the second you sit down to write.

"Who do you think you are?" "You're too old for this." "Nobody wants to read what you have to say." "It's all been done before." "You're wasting your time."

That voice? It's not your truth. It's your inner heckler. And it doesn't deserve the mic anymore.

Where That Voice Comes From

The inner heckler isn't original. It's a patchwork of old criticisms, comparison traps, and cultural nonsense we've picked up over time. A bad teacher. An unsupportive partner. A parent who didn't get it. A toxic critique group. A rejection letter that hit too hard. That one friend who rolled their eyes when you said you wanted to write a book.

The heckler collects these and uses them against you like it's getting paid by the hour. Good news? You don't have to listen anymore.

This part may seem fictional, however, believe me, it's not. Sometimes, in my writing projects, depending on the level of focus or the time needed to meet the deadline, "the Heckler" can't keep up. And it lies quietly. I feel confident, immersed in the writing and what I'm sharing, and when I least expected—there it is. *"Are you sure, this is clear? This is not good enough, try more research...etc."*

I've been writing long enough to know how to respond. I take a sip of my favorite tea, or whatever beverage, depending on the time of day and the subject matter I'm writing about--And tell it to go away. This is a time to manifest ideas into written form. There will be plenty of time to edit the work intentionally. Don't let the inner critic rob you of your flow when the stream of consciousness is flowing into the lake of creativity.

You Can Hear It—But You Don't Have to Obey

The goal here isn't to pretend you never have doubts. Everyone does—yes, even bestselling authors. The goal is to **keep writing anyway.**

Let the voice exist. Acknowledge it. And then… *get back to* work. Try saying this aloud the next time the heckler shows up:

"I hear you. But you don't get to run the show today."

Then prove it. Write the next sentence.

Imposter Syndrome: That Sneaky Voice That Says, "You're Not a Real Writer"

Imposters Syndrome deserves an explanation, as some who may not be in the writing profession may not be aware of this explainable malice. Once you know what it is, you can set it aside, along with all the hesitations we may have had in the past.

I will address this here for those who have written in the past and left it behind as life took over. It also needs to be discussed with those embarking on a writing phase, since it's bound to arise sometime down the road. Even after fifty, even with a few (or a shelf full of) accomplishments under your belt, imposter syndrome can creep in like a shadow at dusk. It's that gnawing feeling that you're somehow faking it—despite obvious signs that you're not.

You might have published a memoir, snagged an award, or heard readers rave about your words—and still find yourself thinking, *"Maybe I just got lucky."* Sound familiar? You're not alone.

Let's break it down:

1. Doubt and Fear

Writers battling imposter syndrome often question their abilities—even when the proof says otherwise. Positive feedback, publication credits, or writing accolades? Somehow, none of it feels like it *really* counts.

2. Downplaying Success

Instead of celebrating hard-earned achievements, writers with imposter syndrome chalk it all up to chance, timing, or someone else's mistake. Talent and effort? They rarely give themselves that credit.

3. The Fear of "Being Found Out"

There's a deep, irrational fear that someone—somewhere—is going to point and say, *"You don't belong here."* The truth? You absolutely do. But that fear can keep even seasoned writers second-guessing themselves.

4. A Common Struggle—Even Among the Greats

Yes, even bestselling, book-touring, award-winning authors have confessed to feeling like frauds. This isn't a newbie problem—it's a human one.

5. What It Does to Us

Imposter syndrome can sap our creative joy, drain motivation, and leave us staring at a blank page. At its worst, it can morph into full-on writer's block.

The takeaway? You're not alone, you're not a fraud, and your words matter—at every age and stage. Writing is not about perfection or permission. It's about persistence, passion, and showing up anyway.

If you've written, you're a writer. Full stop.

Things That Help

- **Recognize the Patterns.** When does your heckler get loud? First drafts? Sharing your work? Naming it gives you power.

- **Write Like No One's Watching.** Because they're

not—yet. You're not writing a Pulitzer on your first try. You're just getting it down.

- **Replace the Voice.** Imagine a cheerleader instead of a critic. Choose your inner Julia Cameron, or Maya Angelou, or Mister Rogers, or your own tough-but-loving grandma.

- **Talk Back (Politely or Not).** Give the voice a name if it helps. Mine is named "Mildred" and she gets shushed with herbal tea and a firm look.

Remember: Doubt Isn't the Enemy—Quitting Is

Every writer has doubts. The ones who succeed are the ones who **write anyway**. Let the inner heckler mumble in the corner. You're here to finish what you started.

Quick Prompt:

Write down one common thought or fear that comes up when you try to write. Be honest. Then write a direct response to it, as if you're talking to a friend, you care about. You'll be surprised how quickly you take your own side when you speak with compassion.

Try This: Give your inner heckler a name. Something ridiculous or oddly familiar. The sillier or more specific, the better. When that voice gets loud, say, "Not now, [Name]. I've got work to do."

Chapter 3
Writing Isn't a Youth Sport

From Frank McCourt to Laura Ingalls Wilder—late bloomers bloom simply fine

There's this unspoken myth in the literary world that if you didn't start writing in your teens, land an agent in your twenties, and get published by thirty, you've somehow "missed your shot."

Let me be clear: **that's nonsense.**

Writing isn't like gymnastics. There's no age cap, no prime years, no risk of being disqualified because you can't turn a back handspring into a metaphor.

If anything, the older you get, the more *qualified* you are. And the literary world is full of proof.

The Late Blooming Hall of Fame

Don't believe me? Let's take a stroll through the Writers Who Started Later and Still Kicked Butt club:

- **Frank McCourt** wrote *Angela's Ashes* at 66.

- **Laura Ingalls Wilder** didn't publish her first *Little House* book until she was 65.

- **Raymond Chandler** published *The Big Sleep* at 51—after working in oil companies for decades.

- **Anna Sewell** wrote *Black Beauty* at 57, and it was the only book she ever wrote.

And these aren't flukes. They're just people who refused to believe that creativity had an expiration date.

Why Maturity Wins

Here's the truth: writing isn't about youthful energy, it's about focus, perspective, and emotional depth. You don't need to write fast. You need to write *well*. And who better to do that than someone who's been around the block (and maybe got lost, fell, came back stronger)?

Older writers tend to:
- Be more self-aware

- Have a better sense of story

- Understand people and relationships on a deeper level

- Care less about trends and more about truth

The Tortured Young Genius Is Overrated

Look, I've read enough pretentious twenty-something writing to last a lifetime. It's not bad—but it's often missing something: **life seasoning**. The kind you earn through heartbreak, joy, aging parents, tough choices, real-world work, and grace under pressure.

If you're reading this and thinking, "Well, I haven't exactly had a dramatic life," think again. You don't need scandal, you need *truth*. And no one tells it better than someone who's lived it.

On a personal note, I believe that my writing would not have the depth that many people attribute to it without the life experiences, diverse background, and various jobs I have held over the years. It is the ability to draw from my past that allows me to write meaningfully in the present.

Currently, I can incorporate thoughts, images, ideas, and knowledge from my diverse journey, which spans modeling and acting, law enforcement, and private investigations. I've also worked as an executive assistant for a fruit and nut brokerage company for over eight years. As a certified holistic life coach, I worked at a rehabilitation facility. I used my skills to help clients gain clarity in their lives and move forward without addictions through art therapy, hypnotherapy, NLP, and other modalities I have studied over the years. However, I continued to write on the side throughout this time, honing my craft while storing these experiences for added substance and depth. And yes, the more you write, the better you get. That is why it is pertinent that you WRITE NOW!

Your life may not be as diverse. Perhaps you attended college, married your high school sweetheart, started a company, and remained there until retirement. In all those years, you undoubtedly encountered hundreds of people—let's call them characters. There have been memorable moments and situations that still make you smile or cringe when you look back on them. Everyone's life is filled with moments to reflect upon. The longer we live on this beautiful planet, the more experiences we must share. Don't you agree?

Quick Prompt:

Make a list of three things you've learned the hard way. Then pick one and write a short scene, memory, or reflection based on it. Don't worry about genre or form—just write from the gut. Really, express what your life experiences brought to the table and how you can add your own spices to make it as flavorful as possible.

PART II:

BUILDING THE WRITING LIFE YOU WANT

Chapter 4
Claiming Your Time and Space

(Because no one's going to hand it to you)
Carving out writing time—even in a busy or retired life. No excuses, just strategy

Here's a hard truth wrapped in love: if you wait for the perfect time to write, you'll be waiting until the next ice age—*and even then*, some woolly mammoth will probably interrupt you.

You're not alone. Whether you're working full-time, retired but busier than ever, managing health challenges, caregiving, or juggling your own circus of responsibilities, time can feel like a luxury you can't afford.

But let me tell you something you already know deep down:

If writing matters to you, you must make space for it.

And not just physical space. I'm talking about mental space, emotional space, sacred space. That tiny pocket of the day (or night) you declare: "This is for me. And I'm not giving it up."

The Myth of "When Things Settle Down"

Spoiler alert: they don't. Not for long, anyway. And that's okay.

Writing isn't about waiting for silence—it's about creating a rhythm in the middle of the noise. It's about showing up, even if the dishwasher is running and the dog is barking. Believe me, the puppies do a job. I have three rescues. So, I know what I'm talking about.

You don't need a cabin in the woods. You need **consistency**, even amid chaos. However, you can write about the Cabin in the Woods. I know that scene sparks a lot of writing prompts and ideas for me.

Finding the Cracks

You don't need hours. You need **moments**. Here's where to look:

- **Early mornings** – before anyone else starts making demands

- **Late nights** – if you're more owl than lark

- **Lunch breaks** – even fifteen minutes counts

- **Waiting rooms** – paper or phone, always be ready

- **Retired or semi-retired?** – make writing a scheduled part of your day, like coffee or brushing your teeth

It's not about having time. It's about claiming it like it's yours—because it *is*.

Creating a Writing Space That Works

Let's talk about where you write. No, you don't need a Pinterest-perfect nook with fairy lights and a reclaimed oak desk.

You need a spot that says: **"This is where I do my thing."** It might be:

- A corner of the kitchen table

- A spare room, even if it still has the treadmill in it

- Your car during soccer practice

- Your bed with a lap desk

- A local coffee shop where 'Mildred' can't find you

Make it yours. Keep a notebook, a pen, your laptop, or even voice-to-text ready. Light a candle, put on music, or hang a "Do Not Disturb (Unless Bleeding)" sign if necessary.

The Ritual Matters More Than the Setting

I have an hourglass on my desk. I turn it over, and I know that's an hour that will be my special creative time. I must admit most of the time, the sand on the hourglass runs out, and I continue writing—because I'm on a roll. I also light a candle, one with lavender, which to me is relaxing but not so much that I fall asleep on the keyboard. It sets the space, it taps into my subconscious, and it sets the intention that is the Right Time to Write Now.

Writing time is sacred—even if it's only ten minutes. The act of showing up builds momentum. And over time, momentum builds pages. Pages build books.

So, schedule it. Defend it. Even if you have to fake a Zoom call to get that peace and quiet, do it.

This may be one of those times when a little white lie goes a long way. Of course, I suggest surrounding yourself with supportive people who have your back when it comes to your dedication to writing. Perhaps, that's a topic for another book.

Because no one is going to hand you time, you must take it.

Quick Prompt:

Write down your current day or weekly routine. Look for one or two pockets of time—no matter how small—where you could consistently write. Then commit to a *realistic* writing goal: 10 minutes? 200 words? One page? Make it yours.

It is better to start with small, obtainable time goals than to schedule a large block of time and fall short of your expectations. Less is more, as it builds the writing muscle. It's like going to the gym or doing a new exercise routine. Suppose you overdo it in the first session. You may not want to do it for another week or ever. Take small steps, and you'll be on the path to a successful and enjoyable writing journey in no time.

Chapter 5
Tools of the Trade (That Won't Make You Feel Lost or Left Behind)

(No tech panic. No eye rolls. Just stuff that works.)
Tech and tools for non-techies. From pen and paper to Scrivener and speech-to-text.

You don't need to be a digital native to be a successful writer. You don't need to be trendy, or techy, or "in the cloud." All you need is a way to get your words down—and keep them somewhere you won't accidentally delete with your elbow.

Whether you're a pen-and-paper purist or open to trying a few apps, this chapter gives you a range of options. No pressure. No judgment. Just tools that *make writing easier*—not more complicated.

Low-Tech Options (They Still Work Wonders)

Let's start with the basics:

- **Notebook and Pen** – Sometimes, this is all you need. Especially for brainstorming or getting unstuck.

- **Index Cards** – Great for organizing plot points or scenes. Shuffle them around on your dining room table and feel like a genius. Or a mystery writer pro.

- **Post-It Notes** – For reminders, inspiration, or "don't forget to write today" guilt trips on your bathroom mirror.

- **Bullet Journals or Writing Logs** – Keep track of word count, ideas, or writing streaks. Low commitment, high payoff.

If you love paper, go for it. Just have a plan for eventually typing it up if you plan to publish or share it.

Easy Tech (That Doesn't Bite)

Not a tech wizard? No problem. These tools are beginner-friendly and useful across all skill levels:

- **Microsoft Word** – Reliable. Familiar. Does the job. Most publishers still accept Word docs.

- **Google Docs** – Free, autosaves constantly, and lets you access your work from anywhere. You can even share it with a friend or editor.

- **Scrivener** – Great for organizing large projects like novels or memoirs. It takes a little learning, but many writers swear by it.

- **Grammarly** – A free (or paid) writing assistant that checks grammar, clarity, and tone. Like spellcheck, but sassier.

- **Dictation Tools** – Use built-in voice-to-text on your phone or computer. Talk your story out, then clean it up later. Perfect if your hands get tired—or your thoughts move faster than you can type.

Bonus Helpers

- **Timer Apps (Pomodoro style)** – Write for 25 minutes, take a 5-minute break. Keeps you focused without burnout.

- **Trello or Notion** – Great for visual thinkers who want to plan chapters, keep notes, or track progress with digital "boards."

- **Calmly Writer / Focus Writer** – Distraction-free writing environments that turn your screen into a peaceful, minimalist space.

- **Backups** – Whether it's Dropbox, Google Drive, or emailing your manuscript to yourself every few days, *please* back it up. Mildred would love for you to lose everything. Don't give her the satisfaction.

Your Tools, Your Rules

Don't let the tech world bully you. Choose what works, what feels comfortable, and what helps you stay consistent. You're not behind, you're building your own way forward.

And for those of you who may not be familiar with the Pomodoro Style, I'm happy to break it down for you.

The Pomodoro Technique: A Simple, Timer-Ticking Trick to Get Things Done

If staying focused feels harder these days—thanks to texts, pets, and the ever-tempting fridge—you're not alone. Enter the Pomodoro Technique, a straightforward time management method that helps you write (or tackle any task) in short, focused bursts. It's perfect for those of us who prefer structure but still need breathing room.

Here's how it works, in plain English:

The Basics

Set a timer for 25 minutes. During that time, you focus—really focus—on just one task. No email, no phone, no folding laundry while thinking about chapter endings. Just the work.

The Breather

When the timer dings, take a 5-minute break. Stretch, sip your tea, check on the dog—whatever helps you reset.

The Rhythm

Do four of these 25-minute work sessions (called "Pomodoro") and then reward yourself with a longer break—15 to 30 minutes. That's your time to recharge before diving back in. If you choose to do so. It's okay if you do one complete session per day.

Why It Works

It trains your brain to work with time, not against it. Instead of feeling overwhelmed by big projects, you break them into bite-sized, doable sessions. You'll stay sharper, avoid burnout, and finally tame that wandering mind.

Make It Your Own

The original method calls for 25-minute sprints, but if you need more or less time, adjust to fit your flow. It's a tool, not a rule.

Where It All Began

Maybe it's me, but I love researching and finding the roots of things in this case something to do with tomatoes. Here is what I found out. My timer is a Penguin, isn't that cool? No pun, I assure you.

Created in the late 1980s by Francesco Cirillo, the name "Pomodoro" (Italian for tomato) was inspired by his trusty little tomato-shaped kitchen timer. Proof that even a humble veggie timer can change how we work.

Try it for your next writing session. One Pomodoro at a time—and before you know it, you're moving that story forward, word by word, tomato by tomato.

Quick Prompt:

Try writing the same paragraph three different ways:

1. By hand   2. Typed into your computer   3. Using voice-to-text on your phone

Which one felt easiest? Which one surprised you? That's your personal writing style speaking. Listen to it.

Chapter 6
Writing Through Real Life

Health, caregiving, memory lapses, or just challenging knees—writing anyway.

Let's be honest—life at this stage doesn't slow down just because we want to write a book. In fact, it might be trying to wrestle the pen out of our hands.

Maybe you're navigating doctor appointments, medications with names that sound like planets, or helping a loved one get through the day. Maybe your joints have their own weather report, or you forget why you walked into a room—let alone the plot twist you dreamed up the night before.

This chapter is for *you*.

Writing now isn't about waiting for the perfect time or the perfect version of you. It's about writing *anyway*. Here's how we do that—with grace, grit, and maybe a heating pad:

Writing With a Body That's Not 25 Anymore

Let's just say it: writing is physical. Your back aches, your knees protest, your hands don't move like they used to. So, adapt the space, not the dream.

- Use voice-to-text tools on days your fingers won't cooperate.

- Get a lap desk, a standing desk, or even write from your recliner.

- Short bursts are better than no bursts at all—remember our spicy tomato friend, the Pomodoro Technique.

Even this technique can be adapted to your unique needs. These are additional things that may help your daily activities and allow for writing time.

Tools to Help You Write Through It
Microwriting: The 10-Minute Sprint

Set a timer for 10 minutes. Write whatever's on your mind. Don't edit, don't overthink. These bursts add up. Five of them a week? You've got a chapter. Be patient, this gets the engine going. Once you make writing a part of your daily ritual no matter what—you'll be able to target your writing to a particular subject or project. Have patience with yourself, you'll get there. In the meantime, enjoy the journey.

The Parking Lot Journal

Keep a notebook in your bag, car, or beside the remote. Use it when you're stuck in a waiting room, watching pasta boil, or avoiding small talk at a kid's soccer game. You'll be amazed how many words live in these in-between moments.

The Permission to Pause

Writing in real life means giving yourself the gift of grace. Missed a day? Week? Month? You're still a writer. Come back in. The chair is still warm and ready for you. No guilt and no judgment, remember you're doing this for yourself. You're the most understanding boss you ever wanted to have.

Make Your Writing Ritual Realistic

A fancy ritual isn't required. If your "writing time" includes a 5-minute rant on paper followed by three decent sentences—win. If it's a voice memo into your phone while walking the dog—win. Make it fit you.

Quick Prompt:

Think about the last ordinary moment that made you feel something—annoyed, peaceful, proud, sad. Write it down in detail. No plot needed. Just capture the truth of it.

Optional first line: "I didn't expect to remember this, but…"

Comfort doesn't mean giving up—comfort means you're in it for the long haul.

Caregiving and Carving Out Time

Taking care of others often means putting your needs on hold. But writing can be your lifeline, your outlet, your few sacred minutes of "you time."

- Carry a small notebook or use your phone's notes app to jot down scenes, thoughts, or dialogue snippets in the in-between moments.

- Set micro-goals—maybe it's 100 words a day. Some books were built that way.

- Don't feel guilty for needing time to write. Writing makes you *more* grounded, not less.

Your story matters, even while you're supporting someone else's.

The Memory May Be Foggy—But the Stories Are Still There

Names, details, even whole ideas might drift away before you can catch them. But don't let that stop you.

- Keep the trusty notebook by your side, I can't stress it enough. It's a life saver.

- Use audio memos to capture ideas on the fly—your phone can be your memory.

- Outline or storyboard your project so you can jump back in even after a break.

You've lived through decades of rich, layered experiences. Your memory might need nudging—but the wisdom is still there.

Permission to Be a Human Writer

Life doesn't need to be tidy to write. In fact, messiness often fuels the most meaningful work. Give yourself grace.

- Can't write every day? That's fine. Just don't quit altogether.

- Feeling overwhelmed? Write what *you* need to hear—it often becomes what others need to read.

- Not every writing session is about producing pages. Sometimes it's about surviving, processing, or healing.

Real Life Is Not a Roadblock—It's the Raw Material

Your aches, your schedule, your caregiving, your "senior moments"—these aren't distractions from the writing life. They *are* the writing life. They add texture, truth, and depth to your voice.

So don't wait for perfection. Don't apologize for the pace. Write from where you are—with humor, heart, and honesty.

And if today your "writing chair" is also your heating pad throne. All the better. The warmth you feel in your body will transcend to your writing voice.

PART III:

THE WRITING PROCESS—FROM IDEA TO MANUSCRIPT

Chapter 7
What do you want to write?

Memoir? Fiction? Nonfiction? A legacy book? A cozy mystery starring your cat? Let's find out.

You're here because there's a story inside you clawing to get out—or at least meowing loudly from the windowsill of your imagination. But before you can write that first sentence, we need to ask one particularly important question:

What do you want to write?

This isn't a trick. It's not even a test. It's a flashlight in the dark, helping you discover what kind of story you're meant to tell.

Let's Talk Genres (No Snobbery Allowed)

Writing isn't a monolith. There's no one "correct" path to follow. Some folks want to author the next Great American Novel. Others want to document their family history so their grandkids will know that Grandpa Joe once wrestled an alligator (or at least an angry dishwasher.)

Here are some broad categories to consider:

Memoir

You've lived. You've learned. You've maybe loved and lost, traveled far, or survived something remarkable. Memoirs are personal, honest, and reflective. It's not your entire life story—that would be an autobiography. Memoir zooms in on a slice: a relationship, an illness, a war, a year that changed everything.

Perfect for you if:

You feel others could learn, grow, or laugh from your story.

You're ready to reflect and be emotionally honest.

Therapy is expensive, and writing is cheaper.

Fiction

Ah, the realm of imagination—where dragons rule and the butler really did do it. Fiction allows you to create worlds, lives, and situations entirely from scratch. Whether you want to pen a sweeping romance, a psychological thriller, or yes, a cozy mystery featuring your cat who moonlights as a detective named Whiskers O'Malley, fiction's your jam.

Perfect for you if:

You daydream more than most.

You like to control the chaos (or stir it).

You enjoy inventing characters and then torturing them for fun and plot.

Nonfiction

This is the big umbrella covering everything from how-to guides and cookbooks to self-help and business advice. If you've got specialized knowledge or a burning desire to help people navigate a particular challenge, nonfiction is your lane.

Perfect for you if:

You want to teach, guide, or share insight.

You have a system, a method, or life experience that others can benefit from.

You'd rather be practical than poetic.

Legacy Book

A deeply personal form of writing that is meant to be passed down to future generations. It's part memoir, part family history, part love letter. Think: the emotional equivalent of a time capsule. You don't need to worry about publishing—this is about preserving your voice and story.

Perfect for you if:

You want your children or grandchildren to know where they came from.

You've collected life lessons like seashells.

You want your legacy to live on in more than just photos.

Hybrid/Other

Don't see yourself in one category? Good. That means you're already thinking like a writer. Your book might be a mix—a memoir with how-to tips. A fictionalized version of your own story. A collection of vignettes or poems. Writing doesn't have to fit into a tight little box (unless you want to market it at Barnes & Noble... then yes, we'll get to that in the publishing chapters).

Still Not Sure? Let's Play a Game.

Ask yourself:

What do I read the most?

What do I find myself talking about at dinner parties (or yelling about at the TV)?

If I had just one story to tell, what would it be?

Do I want to make people laugh, cry, think, or do something?

There's no wrong answer. Just one you haven't admitted aloud yet.

Reality Check

Choosing your genre or form isn't permanent. You can change your mind. You can pivot halfway through the process. You can write a memoir, decide it's too raw, and fictionalize it instead. You're not getting married to a genre—you're dating it. (And if it ghosts you, well... you write a revenge novel.)

At the End of the Day...

The right thing to write is the thing you won't shut up about. The thing you can't stop thinking about. The idea that returns at 2 a.m. or smacks you upside the head and makes you turn the lamp on and reach for your trusty notebook.

Start there.

Time to share:

I am an eclectic writer. The saying "stay in your lane" does not apply to me or my writing. I began my journey with self-help books, but my creativity soon led me to explore other genres. Inspired by my little rescue dog, Chloe, I ventured into children's literature and created an illustrated book. After meeting a lovely cozy mystery author and attending a genre-specific meeting, I decided to try my hand at cozy mysteries. Now, I'm developing a cozy mystery series and adapting the first book into a movie script.

Authoring this book has brought me full circle to my original goal: to help others and share my knowledge, hoping to inspire someone else to try and enjoy it. Believe me, once you welcome the muse, the sky is the limit.

YOUR TURN: REFLECTION & WRITING PROMPTS

1. What kind of book do I feel most drawn to writing?

(Memoir, fiction, nonfiction, legacy, hybrid, or "still figuring it out")

2. What's one story or idea I've carried with me for a long time?

Write it in one sentence.

3. Who am I writing this for?

(Myself, my family, readers like me, a specific person?)

4. What would success look like for me as a writer?

(Finishing the draft? Publishing? Leaving a legacy?)

5. What scares me most about writing this? What excites me most?

Name both. They usually sit on the same shelf.

Chapter 8
From Idea to Outline (or Not)

Plotters, pantsers, and something in between. A judgment-free zone.

You've got the idea. Maybe it came to you in a dream, during a walk, or in line at the DMV (in which case: congratulations, something good did come from the DMV). Now what?

Well, that depends on how your writer brain likes to operate. And here's where we enter one of the most hotly debated—and wildly misunderstood—territories in the writing world.

Are You a Plotter, a Pantser, or a Plantser?

Let's break it down. These aren't Hogwarts houses. There's no Sorting Hat. Just you figuring out your rhythm.

Plotters: The Architects

Plotters love a good blueprint. They map things out—scene by scene, beat by beat. They might use index cards, spreadsheets, whiteboards, mind maps, or software like Scrivener. Plotters sleep better knowing where the story is going. Surprises are for readers, not writers.

Perfect for you if:

You like structure.

You want to avoid getting stuck midway.

You get hives thinking about writing without a plan.

What it looks like:

Detailed chapter outlines

Character bios

Timeline spreadsheets

Color-coded folders (or at least color-coded post-its)

Pantsers: The Explorers

"Pantser" comes from "writing by the seat of your pants." No outline, no roadmap, just vibes and guts. You sit down, put your fingers on the keyboard, and discover the story as it unfolds. For pantsers, writing is an adventure—they need to be surprised.

Perfect for you if:

You get bored if you know the ending.

You trust your instincts.

Planning kills your creativity.

What it looks like:

A blank page and a bold heart

Wild plot detours that somehow work

Mid-draft existential crises (but also some magic)

Plantsers: The Hybrids

A happy medium between structure and spontaneity. Maybe you jot down major plot points or a loose chapter guide. Maybe you write until you get stuck, then outline. It's like packing a few snacks and a rough itinerary for a road trip—you've got a direction, but you might still detour through that weird dinosaur museum.

Perfect for you if:

You like flexibility with a bit of scaffolding.

You need to write some scenes to figure out the story.

You like rules, but also like breaking them.

The Truth? All Methods Are Valid

There's no gold medal for outlining, nor a trophy for winging it. Some bestselling authors outline obsessively. Others never do. Some switch between methods depending on the book, the genre, or the mood.

Think of your writing approach like cooking:

Plotters use recipes.

Pantsers throw stuff in the pan and season as they go.

Plantsers glance at the recipe, then freestyle with confidence.

Write how your brain works best. You're not being graded. You're just trying to finish the thing.

But What If I Don't Know Yet?

Great. That means you're still learning your process—and you're in good company. If the idea of outlining it makes you itch, don't. Start writing. If starting without a plan fills you with dread, then plan first. Try both. Try neither. Just keep moving forward.

Remember: It's easier to steer a moving car than one sitting in the driveway.

Tips for Each Type:

For Plotters:

Don't over-outline to the point of paralyzing your creativity.

Leave room for spontaneity—your characters may surprise you.

For Pantsers:

Keep a running "story bible" as you go, so you don't lose track of names, timelines, or eye colors.

If you stall, try outlining the next three scenes—just enough to reboot momentum.

For Plantsers:

Use flexible tools like bullet points or beat sheets.

When in doubt, write a messy first draft then shape it with structure.

On a personal note:

Personally, I'm all the above; it really depends on the project. It all starts with an idea, and even before that, a desire to share a particular story. Once I have the thought percolating like a good cup of coffee, it develops. If it's a non-fictional self-help or instructional book, I start with a rough table of contents of the topics related to the subject. Believe it or not, the first thing that pops up is the book title. Now, don't think this is a rule. I've spoken to many authors who draft an entire book and then devise the title that matches the subject best.

In the case of my children illustrated book, I had the inspiration from my cute little Chloe. That developed as a series of illustrations. I saw the story take shape with pictures. Once the illustrations were completed, all I had to do was add the words to the story.

When it comes to my mystery novels, I'm a complete Plantser. The theme, plot, and characters flow into my imagination like a captivating movie reel. I sit at my laptop and dive into writing the first scene—the story unfolds from there. The characters come to life, and I give them the freedom to soar. Of course, as the writer/director, I maintain some control to prevent chaos. I treat the writing process like an investigation. I keep a binder where I jot down character descriptions and their qualities. I also keep a reference of the locations. This way, if I use some of the characters in future books, I ensure they remain consistent—hair color, eye color, height—you get the idea.

The reason I'm sharing my style is to show that you have absolute freedom to do what feels right for you. There is no wrong way to write. You can start one way, change your approach mid-course, and do a mashup at the end. As long as you keep writing, your job is done.

YOUR TURN: REFLECTION & WRITING PROMPTS

1. Which writing style do I lean toward—plotter, pantser, or plantser?

(Explain your choice. Have you always written this way?)

2. What tools, if any, do I like to use to organize my thoughts?

(Notebooks, digital apps, color-coded post-its, napkins?)

3. What's one scene or moment I already know will be in my book?

(Write it down. It's your North Star.)

4. What scares me more—writing without a plan or creating the plan itself?

(Explore why.)

5. Do I give myself permission to try, fail, and adjust?

(Spoiler alert: You should.)

Whatever your method, your story needs you—not someone else's process. So, get that idea out of your head and onto the page, one scene, one scribble, one glorious mess at a time.

Chapter 9
The First Draft: Ugly or Not

Not every writer does "messy on purpose."

Whether you dive in clean or scrawl it out, this chapter helps you find your own first-draft rhythm—and stick with it.

Let's get one thing straight right up front: first drafts are not supposed to be perfect.

They're not even supposed to be good.

They're supposed to exist.

That's it. That's their whole job.

But here's where things get tricky: every writer approaches the first draft differently. Some make beautiful, clean sentences on the first pass (and we pretend to like them). Others churn out gloriously messy, chaotic word debris that looks like a literary crime scene. Most of us fall somewhere in between, depending on the day and the caffeine.

Embrace the Ugly (Or Don't—It's Your Process)

The popular advice is: "Put it all out, clean it up later." And for many, that works. You throw the whole lasagna at the wall, knowing you'll sort out the noodles later.

But not everyone thrives in that mess. Some writers need order to move forward. If sentence #1 is clunky, they can't write sentence #2 until they fix it. And that's okay—so long as you don't get trapped in the quicksand of endless tweaking and never make it past Chapter One.

Think of the First Draft As...

A blueprint, not the house.

A test kitchen, not the grand opening.

A first date, not the wedding.

The muddy, glorious battlefield where the real story starts to show up.

What Actually Matters in a First Draft:

Momentum

Consistency (showing up regularly—not perfectly)

Staying curious, even when the plot derails or the characters hijack the story

Getting to the end, even if the ending makes you wince

Nobody's asking you to write like you're being judged by Hemingway's ghost. Just show up.

Find Your First-Draft Rhythm

Ask yourself:

Do I write better with a word count goal or a time goal?

Can I stay in flow if I leave placeholders like [describe this later] or [insert brilliant metaphor here]?

Do I feel better writing one solid paragraph or pages of raw material?

Am I more likely to write daily, weekly, or in intense weekend bursts?

Your rhythm doesn't need to match anyone else's. It just needs to work for you.

Tips for First-Draft Success (Or Survival):

Set small, achievable goals.

200 words a day? Great. One scene per week? Perfect. You don't climb Everest in one leap.

Don't go back and edit—yet.

Unless your soul physically cannot move forward, resist the urge to rewrite. That's a job for Future You (who is braver, wiser, and has snacks).

Talk to yourself.

Literally write in the margins: Not sure if this works or fix this later. Give your brain room to be imperfect now and brilliant later.

Write out of order.

Don't know how Chapter 3 ends? Skip it. Write the ending. Write the fight scene. Write about the awkward dinner party. Stitch it all together later.

Don't compare your draft to someone else's polished book.

That's like comparing your behind-the-scenes to their red-carpet reveal.

Permission Slip (Read This Aloud If Needed)

I, [insert your name here], solemnly swear that I do not need to write a perfect first draft.

I am allowed to write weird sentences, messy scenes, and characters who might accidentally change names halfway through.

I will finish this thing, even if it limps across the finish line in a bathrobe and fluffy slippers.

Because I am a writer. And this is what writers do.

YOUR TURN: REFLECTION & WRITING PROMPTS

1. What's my biggest fear about writing the first draft?

(Name it. It loses power once it's on the page.)

2. Do I prefer writing fast and messy or slow and precise?

(Have I tried the opposite just to, see?)

3. What's one non-negotiable routine that helps me write consistently?

(A cup of tea? Jazz music? Hiding from your family?)

4. What would make writing more fun for me right now?

(Think small. A new notebook, a scented candle, cat-shaped paper clips, dog-shaped paper clips. I have both.)

5. What's one scene, idea, or moment I can't wait to write—no matter how it turns out?

(That's the heart. Write toward it.)

The first draft is the beginning of the real magic. It's where you build trust with your story—and with yourself. So, write it ugly. Or write it beautifully. Just write it.

Chapter 10
Editing without Tears

How to revise without losing your voice – or your sanity

Let's get one thing straight: writing the first draft is hard. But editing? Editing is where most writers either level up—or give up.

Why?

Because once the glorious haze of creativity lifts, what's left behind is the reality of what you actually wrote. And sometimes, that's a mess. A beautiful, promising, wild, possibly incoherent mess.

The good news? That's exactly how it's supposed to look at this stage.

Editing = Erasing Your Soul

Many people fear that editing will somehow "scrub away" their voice. That tightening structure, refining scenes, or deleting fluff will make it sound less like them.

False. Editing doesn't silence your voice. It gives it a microphone and turns up the volume.

Your voice is in the choices—in the details you keep, the tone you shape, the rhythm of your words. Editing helps you get out of your own way so that your voice can shine without tripping over typos or dangling plot threads.

The 3 Phases of Editing (Because Yes, It's a Process)

1. *Big Picture (a.k.a. Developmental Editing)*

Look at your draft like a director watching the first cut of a film. You're watching for:

Structure (Does it flow logically?)

Pacing (Where does it drag or sprint too fast?)

Plot holes (Was Aunt Mabel the maid in Chapter 3 and appeared as the Mistress of the Manor in Chapter 9?)

Character arcs (Are they consistent, compelling, or just there to hold your coffee?)

Ask yourself:

What's missing?

What's in here that doesn't serve the story?

What scenes need more oomph?

Tip: This is the hardest edit emotionally. Be kind but ruthless.

2. *Line Editing (a.k.a. Where the Magic Happens)*

Once the structure's solid, zoom in. You're looking at:

Word choice

Sentence rhythm

Clarity

Tone consistency

Dialogue that doesn't sound like two robots trying to order brunch

Think of this as polishing—not rearranging furniture, but fluffing pillows, dimming the lights, and setting out the good snacks.

Tip: Read it aloud. If it sounds clunky, it is.

3. *Copyediting/Proofreading (a.k.a. The Final Shine)*

This is where you catch:

Typos

Grammar gremlins

Punctuation chaos

Continuity errors (Did the cat's name change from Muffin to Meatball?)

Tip: Do this step last. Fixing commas before the story structure is solid is like painting walls in a house that's still missing half the roof.

How to Survive the Edit Without Losing It

__ Take breaks.

Seriously. Your brain needs rest to spot flaws and find better phrasing. Go walk the dog. Or stare at your cat and contemplate their editing wisdom.

__ Don't try to do all three editing phases at once.

You'll confuse yourself, burn out, and possibly cry into your coffee.

__ Kill your darlings (but keep the body).

You may have heard it before. But remember—sometimes your favorite line isn't right here but might be perfect later. Don't delete it forever. Cut and paste it into a "Darlings" doc and revisit it when you're done.

__ Know when to stop.

No book is ever finished. It's just abandoned at a reasonable stopping point. Set a deadline for edits or you'll tweak commas into eternity.

What If You Hate Everything You Wrote?

Welcome to the club. That's a sign of progress. It means you've grown since you wrote the first draft. You're seeing with sharper eyes.

On a personal note:

There are moments when I stumble upon old files and discover a story I wrote years ago. As I read it, it feels like it was written by someone else—or at least, I hope it was. My initial reaction might be to crumple it up and toss it away, but I resist. Instead, I read it again with fresh eyes, taking a step back to reconsider. The idea might still be valid if I let my inner editor take charge. By allowing myself the time to review it, I realize that it represents a piece of time and space, something that had meaning when it was written. So rather than discarding it, I choose to rewrite it, add some spice, and heat it up. Like leftovers, it might turn out even better the second time around.

Instead of despairing, ask:

What's the heart of this story?

What's worth saving—and how can I bring it into focus?

How would I write this now if I had to do it from scratch?

And then... do that.

YOUR TURN: REFLECTION & EDITING EXERCISES

1. What's one scene or section I already know needs cutting or rewriting?

(Write down why—and how it could be stronger.)

2. Where in my manuscript does my energy start to dip when I reread it?

(That's probably where your reader's attention will wander, too.)

3. What's one line I absolutely love—and one I should probably delete but haven't yet?

(Courage, friend.)

4. Do I need help from a beta reader or editor?

(Who could I trust to give honest, helpful feedback?)

5. What's my editing schedule or routine?

(Are you better with short bursts? Long editing sessions? Noise-canceling headphones?)

Editing doesn't have to be painful. It's not punishment, it's part of the creative process. You're shaping clay into sculpture, blurry snapshot into art.

You already did the hardest part—you wrote it.

Now let's make it stand out.

PART IV:

GETTING IT OUT THERE

Chapter 11
To Publish or Not to Publish?

Traditional, indie, hybrid, or just to the family—there's no wrong way.

You've done it. You've written the thing.

It might be a polished manuscript, a charmingly messy draft, or a family legacy project held together with duct tape and hope—but either way, you've made it to the point every writer reaches:

Do I publish this, or do I keep it private?

Let's start with this truth: not every book needs to be published.

And just as importantly: every book deserves to be respected, published or not.

You may want to hold your story close and pass it down like heirloom china. Or you might want to share it with the world—or at least your cousin Shirley.

Whatever you decide, here's the deal: there's no wrong path. Just the one that feels right for you.

Let's Look at Your Options (No Judgment, No Elitism)

Traditional Publishing

This is the "old school" route. You submit your manuscript (usually via a literary agent), a publishing house buys the rights, and they handle editing, design, printing, distribution, marketing (kind of), and more.

Pros:

Professional editing, cover design, layout

Access to bookstores, libraries, major reviewers

A certain level of prestige (your Aunt Linda will be extremely impressed)

Cons:

Extremely competitive—rejection is part of the game

Often takes years from finished manuscript to bookstore shelf

Less control over cover, edits, title, and timing

Advances are shrinking, and marketing support isn't guaranteed

Best for you if:

You dream of seeing your book on shelves at Barnes & Noble, want access to wider markets, and don't mind playing the long game.

Indie (Self) Publishing

This means you publish the book—either digitally, in print, or both. You can do it through platforms like Amazon Kindle Direct Publishing (KDP), IngramSpark, Draft2Digital, or BookBaby.

Pros:

Full creative control: you pick your cover, editor, title, pricing, and release date

Faster to market—you can publish in months (or even weeks)

Higher royalty rates (typically 60–70%)

Cons:

You handle (and pay for) everything: editing, cover design, formatting, marketing

It's difficult to get your book into brick-and-mortar stores or libraries, at this point. With the growing number of beautifully written books, there might be some changes soon.

If you're feeling ambitious, once your book is published, consider visiting your local bookstore with a copy in hand. Introduce yourself as a local author and engage in a conversation. If you connect with the store owner, you might have the opportunity to collaborate on a book signing event. These events are enjoyable and can be mutually beneficial. The store owner receives a percentage of the books sold during the event, and the event attracts people who may not have been familiar with the store it's a win-win.

Some people still assume self-publishing = low quality (they're wrong, but they exist)

Best for you if:

You want control, have a DIY spirit (or a budget to outsource wisely), and want to get your book into readers' hands sooner rather than later.

Hybrid Publishing

Somewhere between traditional and indie. You pay a reputable publisher to publish your book—but unlike vanity presses, hybrid publishers vet manuscripts and provide professional services.

Pros:

You get professional production and editing

Faster timeline than traditional publishing

More creative say than traditional routes

Can still earn decent royalties

Cons:

It costs money—sometimes a lot of money.

You must vet hybrid publishers carefully (many are great, some are sketchy)

Not all hybrid books are eligible for review or bookstore placement

Best for you if:

You want professional polish but don't want to wait years—or wrestle Amazon alone.

Private or Legacy Publishing

This is for the folks who say, "I'm not trying to be the next Nora Roberts—I just want my grandkids to know where they came from."

You can print a small run of books just for family and friends using print-on-demand or local printers. You don't need ISBNs, distributors, or marketing plans. You just need your story preserved. In case you're not familiar with ISBNs, here is what they are:

An International Standard Book Number (ISBN) is a unique numerical identifier assigned to published books and other book-like products, including audiobooks and eBooks. It serves as a kind of digital fingerprint, allowing for easier identification, tracking, ordering, and sale of books globally.

Pros:

No pressure, no rejection

Personal satisfaction and family legacy

Great gift or keepsake

Cons:

Not for public distribution

You're on your own with editing/design unless you hire help

May still cost money for formatting or printing

Best for you if:

Your book is for the people you love—and that's more than enough.

Choosing What's Right for You

Here are a few questions to help you decide:

Do I want this book to reach strangers or just loved ones?

Am I willing to wait a year or more for publication, or do I want it out sooner?

Do I have the budget (or interest) to hire professionals to help me self-publish?

Am I comfortable learning new tech or platforms (like Amazon KDP)?

Do I crave full control—or prefer a team to take the wheel?

There's no wrong answer—just the one that fits your goals and bandwidth.

Be Honest About What You Want

If publishing sounds exhausting, you're not alone. Writing a book is a massive achievement all on its own. If you choose not to publish, you're still an author.

But if that little voice in your head keeps whispering, "Share it," then maybe it's time to listen.

Remember: You don't need to publish like everyone else. You just need to publish in a way that's right for you.

YOUR TURN: REFLECTION & DECISION PROMPTS

1. Why did I write this book in the first place?
(Hint: The answer can help guide your publishing choice.)

2. What does "success" look like to me?
(Bestseller list? Personal fulfillment? A printed copy in my hands?)

3. Which publishing path sounds most appealing—and most realistic—right now?
(Feelings count just as much as facts here.)

4. What's holding me back from publishing?
(Fear, budget, tech intimidation, not sure where to start? Let's name it.)

5. What's one step I can take this week toward publishing—or deciding not to?

(Look up an indie platform? Research agents? Ask for help?)

Publishing is just the ultimate step in a deeply personal, often transformative journey. Whether you go big, go indie, or go private, the important part is this:

You did the thing. You wrote the book.

And that alone? That's everything.

Chapter 12

Navigating the Publishing World (Even if You Detest Social Media)

Agents, platforms, and promo basics—just the stuff that matters

Let's be honest. You didn't start writing because you dreamed of posting TikToks or dancing with your cat in hopes of going viral. You wanted to tell your story, share your wisdom, maybe pen that cozy mystery with your snarky Maine Coon as the sleuth.

But now here you are, staring down at the publishing world and hearing things like:

"What's your platform?"

"Have you built your mailing list?"

"Do you have a Reels strategy?"

Cue the eye twitch.

Don't panic. Breathe. You've got this.

You do not have to turn yourself into a social media guru overnight—or ever, really. But if you're serious about getting your book out there, it helps to understand the lay of the land. Here's the good news: you can do this in a way that suits you.

Let's Break Down the Options

I know we mentioned this in a previous Chapter, but it bears repeating as it applies to how each option affects your involvement level.

Traditional Publishing

This is the old-school route. You submit your manuscript to agents or publishers, hoping for a contract that gets your book into bookstores and libraries. They usually handle the editing, design, and marketing (but spoiler alert: they still expect you to help promote your book).

Pros: Professional editing, credibility, bookstore distribution.

Cons: Takes time, rejection is part of the game, less control.

Indie Publishing (Self-Publishing)

You're the boss here. You hire your editor, your designer, your formatter (unless you want to DIY), and publish on platforms like Amazon Kindle Direct Publishing, IngramSpark, etc.

Pros: Total control, higher royalties, faster timeline.

Cons: You're the boss of everything. That includes marketing.

Hybrid Publishing

This model blends traditional and indie. You pay for services but get support—sometimes distribution and marketing too.

Pros: Help without gatekeeping.

Cons: Upfront costs. Vet these carefully—some are predators in a trench coat.

Just for Family or Friends

Who says you need a bestseller? Maybe your goal is to capture a family legacy or personal memoir for loved ones. You can publish a beautiful book using print-on-demand services and never set foot on Instagram.

Pros: No pressure, deeply meaningful.

Cons: Limited audience—but maybe that's the point.

About That "Platform" Thing

Publishing folks often want to know: Do people know who you are? Will anyone buy your book besides your Aunt Marge? That's what "platform" means. It's not just about followers or likes. It's about connection.

Are you part of a writing group, book club, or niche community?

Do you have a newsletter list, blog, podcast, or public speaking gig?

Are you an expert in your topic (memoir, nonfiction, history, etc.)?

That's your platform. You can build one authentically—without fake followers or viral dance routines.

Promotion Without Pain

You do not have to be everywhere. Pick what fits.

Website: A simple author site is your digital home base. Add a short bio, a photo that doesn't make you cringe, and links to your book or newsletter.

Newsletter: One of the best tools for connection. Short, simple updates sent occasionally via services like MailerLite or Substack.

Events: Libraries, bookstores, retirement communities, writing groups—real people who will care.

One Social Platform (Optional): If you must dip a toe in, pick one. Facebook is friendly for this age group and more forgiving than Twitter/X or TikTok.

Don't worry about being "everywhere." Be somewhere—where your readers are.

What If You Hate All of This?

Here's the trick: write a terrific book. Seriously. Word of mouth is still the best marketing there is. And if you're genuinely allergic to promo, consider:

Hiring a virtual assistant or publicist (there are budget-friendly ones).

Teaming up with fellow authors to cross-promote.

Asking friends and readers to share.

You don't have to do it all, but you do have to do something. Publishing is not a passive sport.

Writing Prompts & Action Steps

Where do you think your book fits?

Traditional, indie, hybrid, or personal project?

Write down why that path feels right for you.

What parts of promotion do you feel comfortable with?

Would you enjoy writing a newsletter? Speaking at a library? Making bookmarks with your book cover?

Make a brief list of your kind of promotion.

Platform check:

Do you already have a small audience somewhere? Are you connected to readers through your profession, hobby, or community?

Brainstorm 3 ways you can expand those connections—naturally.

Tech-free challenge:

How could you promote your book without ever touching social media?

(Hint: Book clubs, email lists, postcards, print ads, podcasts, radio, word-of-mouth...)

Chapter 13

Rejection, Reviews, and Not Giving a Care

Thick skin isn't required—but perspective is

Here's a universal truth: if you create something and send it out into the world, someone's going to dislike it. Maybe even hate it. Maybe they'll call your book "predictable," "self-indulgent," or "not what I expected—one star." And when they do, it will sting. You are not alone.

First, Let's Talk About Rejection

It starts with submissions: agents, contests, editors, beta readers. You may hear nothing. You may get a polite "not for us." You may get the literary equivalent of ghosted. It doesn't mean your work is bad—it just means that person, on that day, didn't connect with it.

What to remember:

Rejection is feedback in disguise. Not always useful feedback, but a data point. Keep collecting them, and patterns emerge. You'll start to notice what works, what doesn't, and where your writing fits.

Stephen King famously collected rejection slips on a nail until the stack got too heavy. If he got rejected, you're in excellent company.

That's one of the reasons he remains one of my very favorite authors. He never gave up and look at him now. He is not only a fabulous writer in my eyes, but an inspiration.

Now, Let's Talk Reviews (Brace Yourself)

Once your book is out there, the reviews will come. Some glowing. Some weird. Some were written by people who clearly didn't read past the first chapter. Welcome to the internet.

The trick? Don't engage. Not with trolls, not with confusing critiques, and not even with the well-meaning "this was okay, I guess" types. A reader's review is their experience. Let them have it.

Pro Tip: Never reply to bad reviews. Not even in your head. The moment you take a review personally; you're no longer the author—you're the bruised human behind the curtain. Go scream into a pillow. Vent to a friend. Then move on.

But What If It Still Hurts?

Of course it does. You're not made of Kevlar. The key is not to numb yourself, but to get bigger than the pain.

Ask yourself:

"Does this review say more about the reader or about my work?"

"Can I learn anything from this?"

"Will I still want to write tomorrow?"

If the answer to that last question is yes, you're already winning.

You Don't Need a Thick Skin—You Need a Resilient Heart

Let yourself feel it, but don't let it stop you. You're doing something brave. You're putting your thoughts, stories, and soul on paper and offering it to others. That's an act of courage. Not everyone can do it—and many who criticize never even try.

On a personal note:

I must admit, my curiosity often gets the best of me, compelling me to follow it. Yes, I've received questionable reviews, and if the reviewer is brave enough to use their real name, my first quest is to find out who they are. What is their experience and expertise? Are they an author? If they are, I pay attention. I'll do a quick search for their books and see how they're doing. Sometimes, I'll even buy one of their eBooks as a point of reference. This often leads me to understand why they said what they said. Perhaps, besides authoring books, they're professors of literature with professional experience that I can learn from to improve my writing.

Then, of course, there are those who don't use their real name. By the way they wrote the review, you can tell the only thing they've ever written is a grocery list. These reviews are easy to disregard, and I hope they're happy with their achievement. At least, I must hand it to them. That day, they wrote—win.

The main thing about writing is to like yourself throughout the process. My advice, if you're willing to receive it:

Don't take yourself too seriously but be serious about your dedication.

In Summary:

Rejection is part of the process, not the verdict.

Reviews are for readers, not for you.

You don't need armor—just purpose.

Keep writing anyway.

PART V:

WRITING WELL, LIVING WELL

Chapter 14
Writing and Wellness

Posture, mindset, staying energized—because a healthy writer is a productive writer

Let's be honest. Writing may not seem like the most physically demanding pursuit—unless you've ever attempted to untangle your spine after a three-hour writing sprint in a dining chair that should've been outlawed by the Posture Police.

Whether you're penning your memoirs or writing the next great mystery series, your body and brain are part of the creative team. And unlike your muse, they don't take kindly to being ignored.

1. The Posture Predicament: Sit Like You Mean It

Slouching is the silent killer of writers (and promising ideas). Poor posture affects your energy, your mood, and yes, even your creativity.

Quick Fixes:

Use a chair that supports your lower back.

Keep your feet flat on the floor. No, not up on the dog. (Personal note, as soon as I go to my desk to write, one of my dogs beats me to it and goes to sleep under the desk. I must make sure my feet stay planted properly on the floor, to avoid bopping him on the nose with my toes. Even my dogs know what's good for me.)

Raise your screen to eye level. (A stack of cookbooks you never use works fine.)

Take breaks every 30–45 minutes, at least. Or discover your best break time. Your joints will thank you.

2. Movement: The Muse Loves a Walk

Sedentary writers tend to lose energy, with low energy, the ideas get drowsy and go to sleep. If you want to keep your ideas flowing, get moving. A short walk can untangle plot knots. A good stretch might reveal the missing sentence you've been chasing all morning.

Don't want to join a gym? Good. Just walk around your block, dance around the kitchen, or do a few yoga poses that don't require an ER visit.

3. Mindset: You Are Not Too Old, Too Late, or Too Anything

The biggest hurdle for many writers "of a certain age" isn't physical—it's mental.

Thoughts like:

"What's the point?"

"No one wants to read what I have to say."

"TikTok authors are 23 and caffeinated—I can't compete with that."

You're not here to compete. You're here to create.

You have wisdom, lived experience, and stories that no influencer with ring lights can replicate. Own that. Mindset isn't fluff—it's fuel.

4. Nourishment: Feed the Brain, Not Just the Buzz

Writers often live on caffeine and carbs until the manuscript is done or their intestines revolt. Please don't do this.

A little protein with breakfast (not just toast and coffee).

Stay hydrated—dehydration is a known creativity killer. Water is your friend.

Keep a healthy snack nearby. (And yes, one piece of dark chocolate counts as self-care.)

5. Sleep: The Original Creative Hack

Sleep is your reset button. One good night of rest can do more for your writing than three hours of doomscrolling about publishing trends.

Don't be afraid of taking a 20–30-minute nap midday if you can. It does wonders to recharge you and the little gray cells.

If you find yourself editing the same paragraph for the fifth time at 11:47 PM... go to bed. Your brain will finish the job while you dream.

6. Breathe: We do it all the time, but do we do it right?

Taking a deep breath, all the way down to your belly button, can lift you up. Give you clarity, energize you, and make you feel so much better. It is so cleansing. I'm telling you, "Go ahead, take as many as you like, they're free."

If you're tense, a little anxious about beginning to write, getting ideas to flow, or just focusing on the blank page until your mind kicks into gear. Take a few breaths, inhaling through your nose, holding for a few counts, and exhaling through your mouth. For me, five is the magic number. It relaxes me, and at the same time, it energizes me. Try it and see if you like it.

If you have any special needs, such as maintaining stable sugar levels or a medical condition that requires more frequent breaks, it's important to listen to your body and consult your medical practitioner. While I'm not a doctor and can only share what works for me, we all have unique needs and different things that keep us going. One thing we share is a love for storytelling and a commitment to helping each other on this journey.

Chapter Reflection Prompts:

What's one physical change you can make to improve your writing environment?

How do you currently manage writing stress—and what's one new wellness habit you're willing to try?

Have you ever noticed your physical state (tired, hungry, stiff) affecting your writing? Describe what happened.

Choose one "writer wellness" goal for the week—movement, nutrition, posture, or sleep—and track your progress.

Chapter 15

Staying Inspired When Life Gets Loud

Writing through grief, joy, boredom, and chaos. The words are still waiting.

There's a moment—maybe in the middle of a news headline, a personal loss, or the clatter of dishes in the sink—when the writing seems to slip away. Not disappear. Just...fade into the background like a good melody behind too much noise.

Welcome to life. Life, with all its messy, marvelous, maddening volume.

If you're waiting for silence, good luck. If you're waiting for peace, it may come—right after the next interruption. But if you're waiting for inspiration? Don't. Write anyway.

Because the words are still there. They're not afraid of your grief. They're not intimidated by your happiness. They don't need the world to quiet down. They just need you to show up.

Grief: Writing from the Wreckage

Grief is a shapeshifter. It can be sharp or slow. It can be numb silence or tidal waves of memory. When it comes, writing may feel pointless—or it may feel like the only thing keeping you afloat.

Sometimes, grief is like standing on the beach, barely getting your feet wet as the tide gently caresses your toes. You get used to the light touch; you enjoy the scenery you breathe in the salty air. And then a rogue wave knocks you on your bottom and threatens to take you out to sea.

You don't have to write about your grief, but you can write through it. Let the page be the place where nothing needs to make sense. Where your sorrow doesn't need to be explained or dressed up. You can scribble, rant, reflect, or just list the things that hurt. That's still writing. That's still progress.

And someday, that writing might help someone else feel a little less alone.

Joy: Writing When the Sun Is Shining

Believe it or not, joy can be just as distracting as pain. When life is good, it's tempting to toss the pen aside and soak up the moments. And you should. But joy is also rich with detail, color, and character. Don't let those golden hours pass unrecorded.

Keep a small notebook nearby. Capture fragments—laughter over lunch, the way the light hits your windowsill, the unexpected kindness at the grocery store. These glimpses of gladness add depth to your writing, even if they never leave your journal.

Joy deserves ink, too.

Boredom: When the Muse Is on Vacation

Some days, inspiration packs up and goes to Tahiti without telling you. You sit at your desk, stare at the page, and wonder if your brain has been replaced with mashed potatoes.

Perfect. That's when you write anyway.

Write about how boring everything is. Describe the clock ticking. Invent a story about why your cat, dog, or bird (Not judging,) keeps staring into the corner (ghost? plot twist?). Boredom is fertile ground if you dig a little.

Creativity doesn't always start with fireworks. Sometimes, it begins with a yawn.

Chaos: Writing in the Middle of the Storm

You've got laundry piling up, a dentist's appointment tomorrow, your phone won't stop buzzing, and someone needs you right now.

Here's a radical idea: write in the middle of it.

You may only get ten minutes. Take them. You might write in your car, the waiting room, the backyard with a barking dog nearby. That's okay. Writers don't need a mountaintop retreat—they need nerve.

Try this: write one sentence. Just one. If that's all you get today, you've still won.

A Final Whisper: The Words Are Still Waiting

Whatever you're facing—grief or glee, chaos, or calm—the words haven't left you. They're patient. They'll sit in the shadows until you're ready to coax them back into the light.

You don't have to be perfect. You don't even have to be consistent. You just must return. Return to the page. Return to yourself.

Because you are still here. And the story isn't over yet.

Chapter 16
Your Legacy in Words

Why your story, your voice, and your truth matter—especially now.

Let's get one thing straight: you're not "just" writing. You're recording a life. Yours. Even if what you write isn't about you, it has a piece of you in it. Whether you're writing a how-to book or a novel, your words are unique; your energy is one of a kind. You are a special being with a magnificent message to share, no matter what the medium. And you're writing your truth, even if it's embellished behind the characters your imagination creates. Creativity is a deep well, with the coals that, under thousands of years of pressure, turn into diamonds. Your writing, too, can be raw, rough, for now.

Not the filtered, polished version—unless that's what you want. Not the version that fits into polite company or holiday newsletters. But the real one. The you who felt it all, lived it all, and dared to sit down and write it out anyway. Whether you're penning fiction, memoir, poetry, or post-it notes, your words are proof that you were here. That you noticed. That you mattered.

What You Leave Behind

Some people leave behind buildings or companies or complicated pie recipes. You? You're leaving something even more precious: perspective. Voice. Truth.

Your writing might one day be found in a dusty attic or passed through generations. But even if it never leaves your drawer, the very act of writing it is a legacy. You are documenting the way you see the world—a way no one else ever has or ever will again.

That's not just valuable. That's irreplaceable.

It's Not Too Late—It's Right on Time

You don't have to be a bestselling author to make an impact. You don't have to have started writing "earlier." You are not behind.

You're right on time.

Some stories take decades to form. Some truths can only be written with the wisdom that comes from living long enough to see the patterns, the ironies, the full arcs. Age doesn't diminish your creative power—it sharpens it.

You've earned your voice. Now use it.

Who's Listening?

Maybe it's your children. Or your grandchildren. Or a stranger in the future who finds your story and sees themselves in it.

Maybe it's just you—reading what you wrote and remembering something you thought you'd forgotten.

And maybe, just maybe, the person who most needs to hear what you have to say… is still out there. Waiting. Searching. Trying to find proof that they're not alone.

You could be the proof.

Writing is the Monument

You don't need marble statues or bestselling book tours to leave a mark. You've already started.

Every paragraph you write is a brick. Every honest sentence is a light turned on. Every silly story, every tender reflection, every detail you capture—it builds something lasting. Something real.

Your words will outlive noise. They will outlast trends. They may even outlast you.

But they will carry your spark.

Closing Thought:

So, what now? You keep going. You write when the mood hits, and when it doesn't. You give yourself grace, and then you give yourself deadlines. You listen to your voice, even when it trembles. You write your legacy—not to be famous, but to be remembered. Not to be perfect, but to be real.

Because there's still time. And the story isn't finished. And you are exactly the writer the world needs right now. So, Write Now!

About the author

Julie Belmont is an eclectic creative with a passion for both the written word and the visual arts. Whether she's drafting a compelling article, sketching a soulful portrait, or penning a mystery, Julie is—above all else—an artist at heart.

With more than 30 years as a freelance writer, she has written articles, poems, blog posts, short stories, and books—many under her name, some as *Jennifer Rogers*, and others anonymously as a ghostwriter.

Her children's book, *Chloe's Journey*, was inspired by her beloved rescue dog and brought to life with her own illustrations. She's also the author of *Bad Blood in the Bayou: Framed*, the first book in her *LA to LA* cozy mystery series, with the second installment, *Wide-Angle*, soon to follow. Currently, Julie is adapting *Framed* into a TV movie or limited series screenplay.

As a visual artist, Julie is known for her ability to capture the essence of her subjects, be it animal, human, or object, and transform it into vibrant, emotive artwork. She especially enjoys commissioned pieces, where she collaborates with clients to bring their vision to life through her unique creative lens.

Julie's deeper mission is rooted in compassion: she actively supports animal rescues, no-kill shelters, and marine life protection. Creativity is her tool. Through her work—on the page and on the canvas, Julie strives to make the world a more beautiful and humane place.

Acknowledgements

Every book has a behind-the-scenes hero, and for this one, that cape belongs to Michele Amburgey. Writer, intuitive coach, and all-around powerhouse, she somehow carved out time from her cosmic calendar to cheer me on, offer feedback, and help spark the creation of the WRITE NOW! Writers' Group on Facebook.

To Michele—thank you for being the kind of friend who shows up, speaks truth, and radiates light (with just enough sass to keep it real). I'm endlessly grateful for your support, your brilliance, and your belief in this journey.

Want to know more about this multitalented wonder? You should visit her at

https://www.MicheleAmburgey.com.

A Note to you, the Writer

If you've made it here—past the doubts, the distractions,
the "Maybe laters" and the
"Who am I to write."
Because you did something brave.
You showed up. You put pen to paper.
You honored your voice.
Maybe you didn't write every day.
Maybe some pages felt messy or small.
Maybe you stopped and started again.
However, you wrote. That is everything.
Remember This:

Your age is not a limitation. It's your Superpower.
You don't need permission to begin.
You only need the will to continue.
Your words have worth—
Whether they're published, private, polished, or raw.
There is no "too late." There is only "now."
You're right on time.
You're not writing to impress. You're writing to express.
To connect. To reflect. To leave a trace.
So, here's what I wish for you:
May your pen stay curious.
May your pages feel like home.
May your voice grow louder with every word.
And may you never, ever doubt that your story matters.
Because it does.
You do.
And we're all better for the stories you're about to tell.

Julie Belmont

www.ingramcontent.com/pod-product-compliance
Lightning Source LLC
Chambersburg PA
CBHW032043290426
44110CB00012B/930